*T*hank you

My sincerest and great love to my husband, children, family and friends who have been such an amazing support throughout this long process. Without your support this book would never have been possible.

I would also love to thank the families, online parenting and Montessori communities, that I've had the pleasure of working with.

This has been an incredible journey, and I so appreciate all those who have expressed support, made inquiries, and connected with me

about this book.

I greatly appreciate all of you.

 *~ Cherine*

A PRACTICAL GUIDE

to

Montessori & Homeschooling

Copyright © 2017 Cherine Muirhead

DISCLAIMER

Making Montessori Ours
South Dundas
Ontario, Canada
www.makingmontessoriours.com
To purchase other books in this series please visit:
www.makingmontessorioursprintables.com
For further inquires please email us at: makingmontessoriours@gmail.com

Montessori Basics

Montessori Basics

Maria Montessori..
- *Who was Maria Montessori?*
- *Is Montessori a good homeschool curriculum choice?*
- *Books Written by Maria Montessori*

Montessori Philosophy..
- *What is Montessori Learning?*
- *What does Montessori have to do with parenting?*

Planes of Development...8, 9, 10, 1
- *What are the Planes of Development?*
- *What are Sensitive Periods?*

Montessori Terms Defined..12, 13, 1
work, nomenclature, command cards, observation, self correct, extensions, didactic, apparatus,
planes of development, sensitive period, concrete to abstract, work period/cycle, cosmic education,
normalization

The Art of Observation..1

The Art of Discipline..1

Montessori & Fairy Tales..1
- *Did Maria Montessori disapprove of fairy tales?*

Great Lessons...18, 1
- *What are the Montessori Great Lessons, and Cosmic Education?*
- *Can I adapt the lessons to suit our family?*
- *Books resources we added to our Great Lessons?*

Impressionistic Charts 2
- *What are Montessori Charts, and Impressionistic Charts?*

Montessori Materials...21, 22, 2
- *What are Montessori Materials?*
- *Do I need all of the materials to be successful?*
- *What materials can I make?*
- *Does Montessori disapprove of colour?*
- *Why are the material colours, and objects so important in Montessori?*
- *Why are many math and sensorial materials created with ten parts?*

Montessori Materials Storage...24
- *Do I need to have all of my materials on shelves?*
- *Storage Solutions for Materials*

Buying Montessori materials..25, 26
- *Where can I buy Montessori Materials?*
- *The question of shipping materials?*

Buying Montessori Manuals/Albums..27
- *Where can I buy Montessori Manuals?*

Presenting Materials..28
- *Why are material presentations so methodical?*

The Three Period Lesson...29
- *What is the 3 period Lesson?*
- *What is the purpose?*

Work trays...30
- *Why are trays used for Montessori Work?*
- *What are 3 Part Card Trays?*

Montessori Basics

Rugs for Work...31
- *Why are rugs used for Montessori Work?*
- *Why do kids work on the floor?*

Three Part Cards...32
- *What are 3 Part Cards?*
- *What is the purpose?*
- *Can I make these?*

Nomenclature Booklets..33
- *What are Nomenclature Booklets?*
- *What is the purpose?*
- *Can I make these?*

Print Material Making..34
- *Tips for making print materials*

The Montessori Home Classroom...35, 36
- *What does a Montessori Homeschool classroom look like?*
- *Do I need a Montessori Classroom setup at home to be successful?*

Montessori Curriculum...37
- *Does Montessori go by grade?*
- *Does Montessori use testing?*

Montessori at Home...38
- *How can I create a feeling of community that is found in a Montessori class at home?*
- *How much do I put on my shelves?*
- *What do I do if my child doesn't want to do the activities?*

Montessori Homeschooling...39
- *Do I need to be a teacher to use the Montessori curriculum?*
- *Is Montessori for gifted children?*

Montessori Record Keeping..40
- *How does Montessori track my child's progress?*

Montessori vs. Mainstream Education..41
- *What is the difference between Montessori and mainstream curricula?*

Work Books & Printables..42, 43
- *Are workbooks used in Montessori?*
- *What are printables, and how are they used in Montessori?*
- *Printables vs. Traditional Materials*

Montessori Tutoring...44
- *Can Montessori be used for after school tutoring?*
- *Can I start with Montessori and then move to another curriculum?*
- *Can I combine Montessori with other curricula at home?*
- *Can I begin Montessori with an older child?*

Montessori Home Organization...45
- *How do I organize my home to be Montessori friendly, and what does that mean?*

Montessori Toys?...46
- *Are Montessori Materials Toys?*
- *Do I need to buy wooden toys only?*

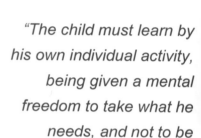

Who was Maria Montessori?

Maria Montessori was an Italian Scientist born on August 31, 1870 in Italy, and became their first female physician. At the age of 28, she became the Directress of a government funded school in a poor housing project. The school was created to educate and support children with varying degrees of social, economic, psychologic, and physiological challenges. Based on research and observation, she developed the Montessori Method and philosophy; along with materials to complement the natural development of children. She worked with many children (in this time period), that were believed to be incapable of learning. The children she worked with in some cases not only performed well, but surpassed the academic standard of *normal* (sadly a term of the time), children. Maria Montessori was an advocate for not only children, but of humanity. She was a brilliant visionary, single mother, and advocate of world peace; that she believed could only be achieved through the gentle, and holistic education of children globally.

Is Montessori a good homeschool curriculum choice for you?

It would be difficult to convince most people who have studied the method, and tried the method in some capacity, that it would not be a good choice. I would encourage you to revisit this question after you have spent some time reading through this book, and conducted further research. You may wish to jump right in, or perhaps you are interested more in the lifestyle and philosophy. Whether you intend to use the method for preschool, or through elementary; it's of great benefit to you and your child, to understand how the entire curriculum and philosophy behind it works. Montessori is at heart about living a connected, respectful life, with your children and family. It's about gaining a solid understanding of your child's natural development, and seeing your child as a whole person, to whom respect is due. It's about gentle parenting, in an effort to see the needs of your children, and to have respect for things that they are passionately interested in. It is also about creating an accessible environment, which we talk about at length throughout this book. Taking a closer look, will help you to determine what will benefit your children and family.

Maria Montessori wrote many books; here is list that we found helpful. Many can be read online for free.

Maria Montessori's Own Hand Book *(Early Materials), By Maria Montessori*

The Montessori Elementary Material, *By Maria Montessori*

The Montessori Method, *By Maria Montessori*

The Absorbent Mind, *By Maria Montessori*

The Secret of Childhood, *By Maria Montessori*

Discovery of the Child, *By Maria Montessori*

To Educate the Human Potential (Cosmic Education), *Maria Montessori*

> *"The child must learn by his own individual activity, being given a mental freedom to take what he needs, and not to be questioned in his choice. Our teaching must only answer the mental needs of the child, never dictate them."*
>
> *~ Maria Montessori*

Image: Dr Maria Montessori's Own Handbook

MONTESSORI PHILOSOPHY

A Practical Guide to Montessori & Homeschooling

What is Montessori learning?

Maria Montessori conducted research while teaching children for many years. She developed materials based on the phases or planes, of natural child development. She created a multi age environment, that enabled children to have complete accessibly and freedom to explore. Key fundamentals of Montessori pedagogy are; respect for the child, following and observing their interests and development, in an effort to foster independence and self-reliance. The early curriculum is a concrete multi sensorial experience, rich with language, and hands on learning. The curriculum is very unique, in that all information and concepts are isolated, and explained in proper terminology to children using realistic images. Maria Montessori was a scientist, so the language and vocabulary used in the Montessori curriculum is accurate scientific language or terminology. This can take a bit of adjustment in the beginning, because most curricula presented in mainstream early years, is generally more limited in information and makes adjustments in vocabulary for different ages; Montessori does not do this.

"Respect all the reasonable forms of activity in which the child engages and try to understand them."

~ Maria Montessori

What does Montessori have to do with parenting?

There are many parallels between Montessori philosophy, and the positive parenting approach; in that children are respected as complete people. There is great emphasis on understanding child development, and what drives behavior. You can certainly read Maria Montessori's Books, however I also found it extremely helpful to read anything I could find about positive and gentle parenting. In addition, unschooling authors have incredible insight into the parent child relationship, and home learning. Unschooling and Montessori share the underlying principles of following the child and their interests. Many teachers during training do extensive work on inner preparation, to help them with this gentle, and respectful perspective toward children; as do most parents. It takes a great deal of strength to see your children for the individual people that they are, and not to place upon them the constraints, and judgment, that we may have grown with as a child. Montessori has shifted in recent years to be more openly reflective of the positive parenting method, in an effort to show those who look to Montessori for guidance online that they are aligned with this practice. Many Montessori teachers also refer to themselves as Montessori guides, rather than *teachers* as some feel that it better reflects the gentle guidance of a child in the classroom. There is certainly a shift to move away from any language used to describe a traditional mainstream class setting.

Image Credit: The Montessori Elementary Material, By Maria Montessori

PLANES OF DEVELOPMENT

What are the planes of development?

Maria Montessori along with many others, believed that a child's development was not a constant linear period or track of growth. There are distinct periods or planes of development, where physical and mental growth were very different. Montessori classified these four planes of development in a graphic, to help visualize the stages of human development; in relation to the mainstream global educational structure.

This is a much deeper conversation, than for instance recognizing the age that a child is most sensitive to receive language (as important as this is to recognize). She was also referring to how we educate children in our mainstream social culture, and it's drawbacks.

The 4 Planes of Development Chart
The Constructive Rhythms of Life

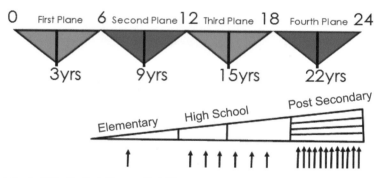

That created and published by Maria Montessori in 1950

The original is difficult to see so I have created a version for you to take a closer look.

"There are different types of psyche and different types of mind at different periods of life. These periods are clearly distinct from one another. It is curious to say that these periods correspond to different phases in the development of the physical body."

~ Maria Montessori
The Absorbent Mind

(free to read on The Internet Archive Library)

The red areas are described as extremely active, and perhaps more turbulent periods; while the blue are considered more calm and steady periods. There is a great deal more to the chart in terms of meaning. The secondary portion shows development along aside progression in the school system. She describes that phases of mainstream education, correspond to human phases of mental growth; meaning a child at 6yrs is most likely able to sit quietly and listen thus being school age etc.

PLANES OF DEVELOPMENT

A Practical Guide to Montessori & Homeschooling

What are the planes of development?

Maria Montessori notes the first period of development is between birth and 6 years of age; the *Period of Creation* in which the child has an unconscious mind. Meaning that a child is born with great instinct and capability, to learn and absorb the environment around them. Language and physical movement are achieved during this period. She also refers to this as *"The Absorbent Mind"*, being the period that a child's mind and processes are literally building themselves, through the absorption of their environment.

"it is not a small creation that the child achieves. It is the creation of all." Maria Montessori, The Absorbent Mind

During the first 6 years of growth, a child will have achieved a level of learning and understanding, <u>equal in proportion</u> to their adult years.

Maria Montessori so keenly conveyed respect for children, and their right to a free accessible environment, right from the beginning.

She subclasses this period into 0-3 years at which she says:

" there is no school for such children." Maria Montessori, The Absorbent Mind

Birth –1yr A child comes to recognize and remember all things in their environment, they instinctually explore and experience their environment through their senses.

The next subclass is 3-6 years of age at which she says:

"this period is characterized by great transformations - at six years the individual becomes" Maria Montessori, The Absorbent Mind

This is a period of conscious development; where a child will put into practice the development and skills they have acquired from 0-3 years with great intension. They will also acquire a great deal of language in this period, as this is the sensitive period to acquire language.

Maria noted that children during this period have tremendous unmatched capability to receive and remember proper terms and words. Thus you will find correct scientific terminology used not only later in the curriculum, but most certainly during very early education.

"Our job is not to teach, but to help the absorbent mind in it's work of development ."

~ Maria Montessori

The Absorbent Mind

(free to read on The Internet Archive Library)

What are Sensitive Periods?

The Second period is 6-12 years of age at which she marked physical changes in growth, such as loosing and growing our adult teeth. Montessori refers to this as a period of physical growth, and also of calm and serenity, in contrast to the previous period. The child is putting all of the knowledge and confidence, in their own ability to work.

This is the period that the child makes the transition from concrete, to abstract learning. This is a period of tremendous growth, in that the child is so open to the world, new ideas and understanding. They are great seekers of knowledge. They have experienced the physical growth and strength to be independent, and in control of their path.

The Third Period she describes as being between 12-18 years of growth in which she says...

"a period of such transformation that it reminds us of the first (3-6) period. This is a period of creation." Maria Montessori, The Absorbent Mind

This period is also marked by the physical and mental changes, occurring during puberty.

This period is sub categorized by 12-15 years, and 15-18 years. At 15 -18 years physical changes are marked, in that the body reaches physical maturity.

This is the period in which the child makes the transition from childhood, to the beginnings of adulthood. Social and societal connections are being formed. They're character and personality, are coming to the forefront. This is as a difficult period to balance due to the rapid changes in all round development that can also be emotional and turbulent. This is a period where great care must be taken, because the child is seeking self-assurance and independence, but also has a great need for connection. This is a period where your child needs to be recognized for the person that they are becoming, and it's vital that they are supported and accepted.

"There are doubts and hesitation, violent emotions, discouragement and unexpected decrease of intellectual capacity" (Maria Montessori From Childhood to Adolescence)

It was for the period of High School that Maria Montessori proposed Erdkinder "Land Children". This was described as a farm like environment in which the child could work and learn, thus building new skills, confidence, self-assurance, and belief in oneself.

The fourth period being 18-24yrs. Essentially, this is described as a period in which physical growth has concluded, and the person will now make their way to work or further study. Maria Montessori refers to the period of University Studies. The world is a very different place now, and this path can mean very different things.

"The human individual constructs a unity when the hand is working and the mind is guiding it."

~ Maria Montessori

The Absorbent Mind

(free to read on The Internet Archive Library)

Sensitive Periods

It is interesting to read her thoughts on mainstream global education, and how so much of what she describes still holds true decades later. In most mainstream educational institutions, education begins at 6 years of age. There has been a fairly recent explosion and movement in terms of the "education" of children 0-6 in the home. It is incredible and has led to amazing movements in parenting, resources, and products for children. It has also become an industry, and is all amazing to see unfolding.

Maria describes a global system of education that is solely based on those who have the mental capacity to sit, and listen, and be dictated to; readiness for education is based on this. It has historically been a system based on conformity, whereas developmental needs, mental growth, and independence are of lesser consideration. This has created huge gaps in terms of equal education.

This system of global education and thinking has really created a condition of dependence, lack of self-esteem, and social conformity. It's not been a system of tolerance for all, because it was built around the basis of conformity. It was a system designed to educate those who were able to sit and receive, and to provide little in the way of interruption, disruption, or specialized need.

The system has stayed in this loop for so long, that it is hard to change it. There is a great deal of discussion, ideas, and thought happening to try and revision and rework public education, in terms of inclusivity of all of humanity. Education is not only for the few who are able to fit the age old model of education; thus so many have made the move toward home education.

Being in the home learning community, and also knowing many who are in the system; it's difficult to watch the struggle of those who are fighting so hard for change including parents, and also many teachers. It's also difficult to watch how little has changed overall, and how slow the process is. I think that a change must be adopted by all, and sadly it is not. Education is also a money making global industry, and many wish to keep it that way; yes many Montessori schools even fall into this trap. I think Maria Montessori would have a good deal to say, about how processed her methods have become in many cases. Many talk the Montessori talk, but are certainly not walking the walk - so to speak.

The only thing that I was ever concerned about, was respecting the growth and development of my children. Was I learning to talk the Montessori talk, or was I actually hopping in with them and walking the walk?

"man himself should become the centre of education.

Man does not develop only at the university: man starts his development at birth."

~ Maria Montessori

The Absorbent Mind

(free to read on The Internet Archive Library)

MONTESSORI TERMS

A Practical Guide to Montessori & Homeschooling

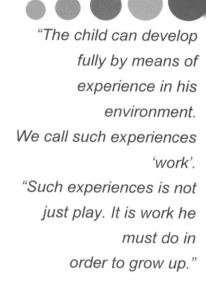

What does it all mean?

Work

Maria referred to a child's play and interaction with their environment as "a child's work". You will most often hear all things related to a child's activity, as their work. This is how a child constructs their own being, and development.

Nomenclature

You will see the word nomenclature a lot, and it simply means a collection of things belonging to one particular topic. You will see a vast number of nomenclature cards and booklets, available for everything from fruit to instruments, to parts of the human body.

Command Cards

Command cards are simply a card, with written instruction for the student. They are activity/lesson cards.

Observation

This is a hugely important word that you will see and hear associated with Montessori, in that Maria believed we needed to stand back, and let a child do their "work". Our job was to observe their actions, and through this we would gain tremendous understanding and direction, in terms of the needs of the child; you must observe to actually truly *see* the child.

Self Correct

Self correct is a measure taken, such that a child can recognize and correct their *own* work. For example, matching activities like Sound bottles and Smelling bottles, may have colored stickers on the back denoting pairs. There are also visual self correct measures like differences in size, as is the case with the Pink Tower. A material like the Spindle Boxes has a specific number of sticks/spindles for the activity, thus if there are spindles left over (or not enough), it is evident to the child that adjustments need to be made to their calculations.

Extensions

You will often hear "extension work" mentioned throughout the curriculum. Extensions are work/activities, created to further enhance additional material use. Many sensorial materials have design extensions or patterns, that can be created with the materials.

"The child can develop fully by means of experience in his environment.
We call such experiences 'work'.
"Such experiences is not just play. It is work he must do in order to grow up."

~ Maria Montessori

Didactic

Maria referred to her materials as "didactic materials". Didactic means materials intended for teaching.

Apparatus

Maria Montessori referred to her materials as the "apparatus", with which the children will experiment. She was a scientist and thus much of the language you will find she used will be reflective of this.

Planes of Development

Four Planes or phases/periods of time during human development that Maria Montessori classified as being 0-6 years of age (sub-classed 0-3 and 3-6), 6-9, 9-12, 12-18. These are periods in which significant changes occur in the physiological, and psychological development of children.

Sensitive period

Maria Montessori referred to phases of growth (planes of development), in which there are sensitive periods that children will most likely seek to learn, and absorb certain skills during childhood development.

Concrete to Abstract

All Montessori materials and curriculum begin with sensorial and motor development. This is a fully hands on experience, in which the child learns by means of exploration and interaction with their physical environment. Thus the materials can be held, experienced physically, evaluated, and measured by the child; this is a "concrete" experience. Later as the child grows and develops greater internal understanding, the learning becomes more abstract; your child will process concepts that they cannot readily, or physically see. For example "feeling and holding the largest block", later your child will discern and evaluate information based on their knowledge of the physical environment that they have collected, through growth and exploration.

Work Period or Cycle

Maria Montessori believed that a three hour period, or cycle of uninterrupted time, created a reasonable window for a child to be able to carry out their desired activity, or work in class. Periods of time when your child is in complete concentration is so vital to development, and if at all possible should not be broken. When you are at home you can exercise this concept even further. Schools function on schedule for a reason, and at home you can create your own formula (should you wish), based on observation of the needs, and interests of your child.

"Knowledge can best be given where there is eagerness to learn, so this is the period when the seed of everything can be sown, the child's mind being like a fertile field. "

"The child becomes a person through work."

~ Maria Montessori

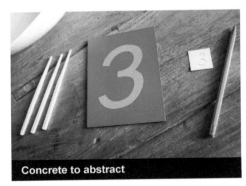

Concrete to abstract

MONTESSORI TERMS

Cosmic Education

Maria Montessori believed in the importance, of a child fully understanding their place in the universe. Understanding the science of the universe, and the world in which we live, are all vital to our sense of global and universal community, and contribution toward world peace.

Normalization

Maria Montessori describes characteristics that have been used to classify the behavior of children "*as soon as a child became interested in work that attracted his attention. So-called bad traits, and the so-called good, all disappeared.*"

Children during her time were classified (and often today as well but perhaps with a little more socially acceptable language) as "good" (social, obedient, well mannered), and "bad" (anti-social, out spoken, uncontrolled physical behavior).
This is a chart created by Maria to visually explain described desired behaviour that the majority of society expresses as acceptable from children. She characterized behavioural "normalization" occurring when a child is engaged in "work" (activity) that is of interest to them. Arguably cancelling out these behaviours, and that every child has the developmental and human right to experience. I have added in brackets a few words to help clarify meaning.

She describes this way of thinking as a social epidemic, in that those who do not fall in the so called "normal range" of behaviour are often ignored, and go without help. As do those who fall in the gray highlighted area, because they are those whom society feel needs no help. This does nothing but further the rise in mental health decline, but also crime rates later in life. She felt that society, schools, and institutions, were in need of great reform. Today her words and findings are more relevant than ever.

"the mind of man is a flame, an all-devouring flame, it is never still, but always active."

~ Maria Montessori
The Absorbent Mind

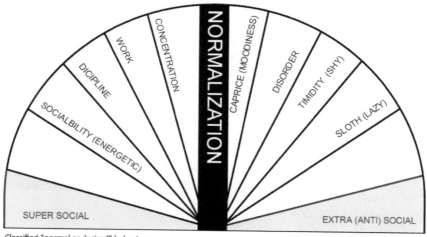

Classified "normal or desired" behaviour

Classified "deviant" behaviour

The Art of Observation

This is the art of observing a child who is deeply absorbed in a moment with complete concentration and intent on mastering the work they have at hand is the heart of the method. This is a very deep conversation that is one of the core principles of the Montessori philosophy, and is perhaps one of the hardest concepts for parents and teachers/guides to grasp. These are the moments where we need to pull back and see our children for the people that they are; that they are doing their natural work to build themselves in mind, body, and spirit. Maria Montessori suggests that teachers who began work in her classroom have had a more scientific background, more readily grasped the art of observation; given it's scientific roots. Observation requires that we do not readily interfere, and allow the nature of the child to unfold. Maria Montessori speaks at length about observation and a great example that will help you so clearly to understand can be found in *The Montessori Method* that begins on page 86 under the chapter of *Discipline*. She describes training new teachers in their first days in her classrooms; "*training is especially necessary for those who have been accustomed to the old domineering methods of the common school.*" She describes the principles of observation as being one of the most difficult to put into practice, and I so feel this is true of any adult or parent. She offers stories of events with the children in class; she describes a small boy who wishes to see what is happening with the older students who are playing at a water basin with boats. She observes this boy scanning the environment for a solution to help, and he intently fixates on a chair and triumphantly begins to climb in effort to see the boats. She observed that the boy had acted on his own accord and looked to himself to devise a solution and acted upon it. This is a huge moment of growth and accomplishment, however the teacher swooped in and grabbed up the child without observing all that he'd just accomplished in those precious moments.

Observation at home can become even more complicated due to all of the daily tasks and rushing that happens in our environments. Maria described a child in a piece that she wrote called *The Mother and Child in 1915*. A child is working intently and quietly putting on his coat to go to the park. He is taking his time contemplating and practicing this practical task with great concentration. Mother (or other grown person) comes along and grabs the work from his hand to get it done quickly, and scoops up the child to hurry him out the door... to go enjoy the park. This action has told a child many things, but mostly that he needs to rely on an adult because he is not capable. We so often want and hope in our hearts for our children to become confident self-reliant grown people, but actions like this rob a child of not only respect but the opportunity to build those precious skills. We worked to slow down and give ourselves and our children the grace of precious time. She has given many examples and here is another that is more directed at the prepared environment or having an accessible home. She spoke of a small child in need to pick things up, to sensorially explore his environment, and he is repeatedly told to stop picking things up and to put them down "don't touch". Observing and *seeing the child needs*, reveals his need to have interaction and freedom to explore. We made the decision to place things that we did not wish to be broken up high or away. The philosophy of "*he needs to learn not to touch*" is a lesson that can come much later. The child's growth and development are dependent upon exploration and creating an accessible space rich with invitations of materials and activities for your child to explore are key.

"life acts of itself to divine it's secrets it is necessary to observe it and to understand it without intervening."

~ Maria Montessori
The Montessori Method

The Art of Discipline

Maria Montessori describes discipline as the liberty or freedom of a child; an act that is developed within, and does not come with imposed external discipline. When we think about discipline today, for some it often looks like outer actions that we must take to ensure our children perform in a desired way. Discipline and observation walk hand in hand, and so often if we slow down and *see our children* in an effort to help prepare an environment that will meet our child's specific needs and importantly their stage of development the idea of discipline will completely change.

It can be such hard work to see your child as a growing person who is at a stage of development or plane that is completely appropriate for them. Meeting your child where they are through observation, and in creating an environment where they have freedom and liberty are key. Freedom of choice in terms of food, dressing, and more importantly precious time to carry out their work are the foundations for developing independence, and self-discipline. Self-discipline is difficult to develop in a constricted environment, with limited choices, with a hurry up and act like an adult feeling that is lingering beneath the surface. We mindfully chose where we decided to go and what we decided to participate in as a family. There were certain situations that were not conducive to the stage our children were at, and we could either choose to embrace this or place a wall of resistance between us and our children. We also altered our expectations and worked to focus on our children and their needs, as opposed to looking to those around us for validation.

Living with your children through observation and liberty in their environment are so transformative as a parent.

"observation has for it's base the liberty of a child; and liberty is activity. Discipline must come through liberty."

~ Maria Montessori
The Montessori Method

Did Maria Montessori disapprove of fairy tales?

This is an interesting subject to explore in Maria Montessori's writing. First off, I think we need to consider that she lived through very distinct periods in time, where children were seen extremely different (in many cases), than they are today. There were many attitudes and phrases to describe children; in that they should be quiet, well behaved, and seen but not heard. Children were to be entertained, and were not capable of great understanding, or complexity of thought, and language; this is sadly seen even today.

Children were to be entertained; thus the development of an entire culture of stories, and products to appeal to children. Stories in some part adopted an undertone of moral teachings, and some toys over time developed somewhat of an educational component or consideration.

Maria Montessori studied the behavior and development of children, and along with others in her time brought forth a revolution for the child. She wrote about the extraordinary unparalleled mental capabilities, of the small child in the first period of development. She talked about the small child's insatiable quest for knowledge and ability to absorb (thus the absorbent mind) information and language; if those in care of them were willing to impart their experience and time, in an effort to share it with them.

I definitely understood from her writing that she felt above all else, that the capability of the child needed to be recognized, and knowledge to never be dulled down or withheld from them due to their age. Thus proper scientific language, and great depth of materials were offered to the interested child.

Children have in depth questions, and it's sad if they go unanswered. This was a certain fact that led our family to Montessori, in that our son had an amazing number of questions and complexity of thought. Montessori presentations and materials met his needs.

Maria Montessori helped to bring about a new understanding and respect of children, and this I think is more the focus to take away from this writing today. I love that today we have access to brilliant materials, to help bring to light knowledge and discoveries with our children. I love that today it is becoming common place, to offer real tangible answers to the questions our children are asking.

As for fairy tales... I feel that most of us now know the value of a child's intellect, and the value of amazing real life experience. I also feel that we all understand the importance and value, in imaginative open ended story based play.

I feel that our world of real life knowledge and resources, have transformed to meet the needs of our children, but that this has also transformed their world of fairy tales and play. I understand what Maria Montessori was saying, and thankfully she has been heard. I feel this is far less about the rejection of imaginative play, as it is about a celebration of the limitless capabilities of the child.

"Does the mind of a child limit itself in taking in objects and facts about things they can see? No; the child has a type of mind that goes beyond concrete limits. Is has the power of imagining things."

~ Maria Montessori
The Absorbent Mind

GREAT LESSONS

What are the Montessori Great Lessons?

The Great Lessons are an integral part of what Maria Montessori referred to as, a child's Cosmic Education. Cosmic Education begins in the 6-9 Elementary curriculum with the introduction to the Five Great Lessons.

These are a set of five Elementary Lessons presented at the beginning of elementary study years, which are usually repeated yearly. They tell the story of the beginning of the Universe, Coming or Beginning of Life, Coming of Humans, Story of Language (communication in signs, story of writing), Story of Numbers. The Great Lessons offer a historical and scientific overview of the universe, and our place in it. In the curriculum the lessons are presented in story form, with a series of experiments and/or activities for each. The story for each as written by Maria Montessori, can be found online for free from many sources, and also found in most Montessori Manuals. Each story is an introduction into deeper elementary study in the areas of Science, Biology, Botany, Zoology etc. They are presented at the beginning of the year, or for homeschoolers when your children are ready and interested. Human History and development are heavily woven into geometry lessons, language, and geography etc.

Can I adapt the lessons to suit our family beliefs?

Yes the lessons can be adapted to the materials you have, and to your beliefs as a family; many adapt the lessons and timelines.

In addition, you may wish to combine more than one lesson, or add in your own materials resources, books, videos, and museum visits to suit your family needs.

Maria Montessori was incredible, in that she believed a child needed to have a very clear understanding of where they came from, as a basis for all future study and questions.

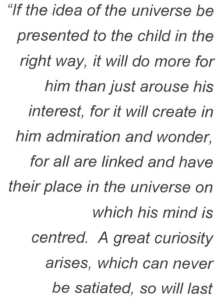

"If the idea of the universe be presented to the child in the right way, it will do more for him than just arouse his interest, for it will create in him admiration and wonder, for all are linked and have their place in the universe on which his mind is centred. A great curiosity arises, which can never be satiated, so will last through a lifetime."

~ Maria Montessori

Coming of Life on Earth Time line

Exploring the History of Writing

Book resources we added to our Montessori Great Lessons

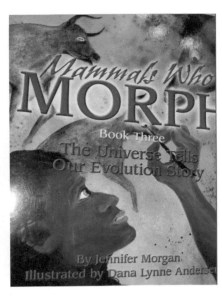

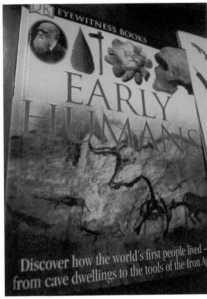

IMPRESSIONISTIC CHARTS

What are Montessori Charts, and Impressionistic Charts?

Impressionistic chart; simply means they are representations of concepts in one image/ graphic i.e., the water cycle chart. Charts or graphics like this have memorable impact (leaving a memorable impression), and are a very valuable tool to help your child visualize concepts. Charts are used throughout the Montessori curriculum, and are used to isolate concepts for children in the form of small poster size images for class use. In the time that Maria Montessori was creating her curriculum, beautiful graphic charts that could be used to demonstrate concepts and ideas to children in class was quite revolutionary. Today these materials can be found in a huge variety of multimedia materials, from retailers, online, and in videos. At home you can decide what makes sense for you to use. The thing that sets Montessori apart, is that the charts are very clearly illustrated; with nothing else to provide distraction from the concept itself. Some charts are accompanied by a story, and others are accompanied by 3 part cards, definitions, and booklets.

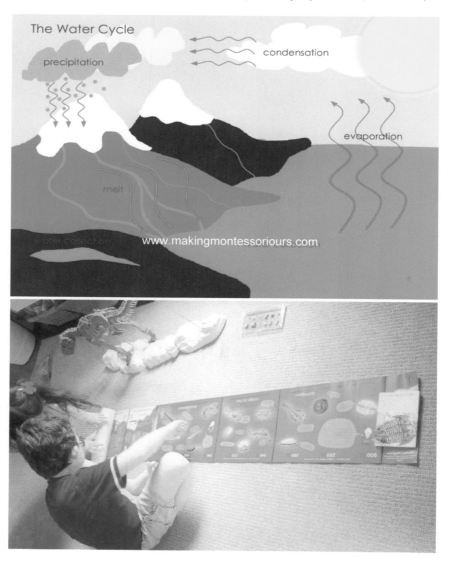

MONTESSORI MATERIALS

What are Montessori Materials?

Maria Montessori developed a brilliant curriculum based on child development with support materials for a child to interact with, explore, and evaluate. The materials she created work together with great purpose to engage a child senses, develop fine and gross motor skills, all while developing a rich vocabulary of language. Montessori is a holistic approach to education, given that it's deeply connected to your child's natural development, needs, independence and choice; thus the connection of the whole child. The in-depth procedure and use of the materials, adds an additional component to the direct purpose of the material; in that the methodical approach helps your child to practice patience, and organization.

" control of error lies in the material itself, and the child has concrete evidence of it."
~ Maria Montessori
Maria Montessori's Own Handbook

Do I need all of the materials to be successful?

Some would say yes, but in my opinion and from our experience, I would definitely say no to this question. You know your child/children best, and are not creating an environment for an entire classroom of children, with individual needs in your home. You may choose to purchase just a few materials, that you feel will most reflect the needs and interests of your children; herein comes the ever present truth of following your child. This also depends on what you already have at home. We were gifted many of our traditional materials, but in truth had great alternatives for early materials already in use in our home. One of the most important things to remember, is not to get caught up in the hype of what you are seeing online. Though no one could have made me see this in the beginning. If you can and wish to purchase all of the materials then that is completely your choice. We have loved all of our materials, but again this need not be the case to be successful. Understanding the principles, parenting, and philosophy of what Maria Montessori was trying to achieve, by far exceeds the materials themselves. What she was trying to achieve was an environment of experimentation and freedom that was fully accessible to the child, so they could develop at their own pace in their own natural way and process. The materials and toys that you make available at home, will aid this process. When you look at the scope and sequence of materials you can determine what will work for you and make sense for you in your home.

What materials can I make?

Throughout this book I will show you everything we have made, and how we made it. I will explain why we decided to make certain materials, and which ones we felt were easier to purchase. Also what these materials do for your children, and what they did for our children. Another amazing thing is that many traditional materials retain good value and can be sold, if kept in good condition down the road to help recoup the cost.

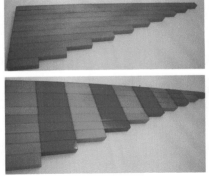

Does Montessori disapprove of colour?

No, and quite the contrary actually. Montessori materials are anything, but devoid of bright colour. I think where you see a more subdued neutral palette is in the envelope of a classroom; meaning that the background of the environment in terms of furnishings and walls, create a quiet backdrop to allow these brilliant materials to have great focus and presence.

The majority of materials are bright and colourful throughout the curriculum, as you can clearly see in the image to the right. Though you can choose certain materials in a neutral wood finish, the way in which colour is used in the Montessori curriculum is interesting and so very important. You also may have noticed that the majority of materials are one solid colour per material, with the absence of visual pattern; and there is a distinct purpose for this. Montessori is widely known for materials that isolate concepts, in effort to help create focus and continuity. Early materials like the Pink Tower is solid pink, such the child can clearly visually distinguish the size difference in blocks. Your child will also innately rely on their senses to evaluate the materials, and to assemble them as opposed to perhaps just matching colours in sequence through memory. It's also a valuable tool in terms of classroom (or home) organization, in that the individual parts of the materials are distinct and easily recognized to be organized together in their home. Variation in colour; as seen with the Numbered Rods, Continent Globe and puzzles, are still solid and minimal to isolate distinct parts. In the case of continent materials the solid colours highlight the shape, form, and diversity of the continents.

This adds to the general debate about brightly multi coloured toys for children, in that they can distract from the purpose. You will need to explore what works for your child, in terms of the toys they are using and the purpose. We had many beautifully made colourful toys in our home that were tools of exploration for open ended design, and creation. We also have our Montessori materials, and in the eyes of our children they were unlike any other toy that they owned, but they interacted with them for their beauty, and interest.

Why are the material colours and objects so important in Montessori?

Think back for a moment and try to remember anyone who you may have heard state something like the following… "Why is it that my child can remember the names of every action figure, but can't remember (whatever that may have been)". There is great power in connecting objects or things, with names or vice versa. This is to a great extent why Montessori materials are object based, and so brilliant. The grammar symbols are a great example of this; when I think about a "noun" I immediately think about the black pyramid, and this is such a strong and powerful association. My child can remember her action figures so distinctly by sight, and remembers their names as soon as she sees them. Objects and physical representations of concepts and words, have great power and lasting presence. This is precisely why language, math, and other subjects are so powerfully presented with objects. This is also why children have such a strong connection to games.

MONTESSORI MATERIALS

A Practical Guide to Montessori & Homeschooling   **Montessori Basics**

Why are many math and sensorial materials created with ten parts?

This is a very simple, indirect introduction of the base ten system of numbers, for your young child.

Your child will begin working with sensorial materials that often have ten parts. They will begin counting in numbers 1-9, with an introduction to the concept of zero. All of their Montessori materials will follow this pattern for a period. When they are well acquainted with units, they will be introduced to a wave of new materials in teen numbers. This is the gateway to the discovery, of patterns in numbers, and this is also why the base ten system is introduced in Montessori a little differently that in mainstream education. Your child will begin by having a solid concrete understanding of place value. The pattern of base ten has been established at this point, and the child is introduced right away to place value unit - thousand, because it makes sense to do so with the concrete materials. This will help your child to concretely understand, a much clearer picture of our number system right from the start.

Do I need to have all of my materials out on shelves?

This completely depends on you, and the storage you have available. You may choose to purchase just a few materials, that you feel will most reflect the needs and interests of your children at a given time.

Many classrooms start with a small selection of materials at the beginning of the school year, and as time and lessons progress additional materials are added. Many homeschool environments rotate materials on their shelves weekly, or on a monthly basis. The ability to do this, depends on the extra storage space you have to contain all of the overflow materials.

Some advise... that you begin slowly with a few appropriate materials, and simply add and change materials with your child's needs and interests; I like this option.
It is overwhelming and very difficult to accumulate all of the materials at once, and to find the needed space to store it all, and I fell into this camp. I used very tall shelves in the beginning, and kept current work on the bottom shelves for accessibility and overflow work above. I did not have an available closet or other means, to store all that I had accumulated. I was very quickly overwhelmed with the size and number of materials in our first Montessori space, and we moved the room to a spare bedroom with a large closet to store materials not in use. I will talk about the evolution of our spaces, and storage solutions that worked well for us in "Our Homeschool Room Section". Keep in mind that at home you need only have the materials available for your children that meet their interest and development; while in a class there are many children in a range of ages to accommodate.

Storing Montessori and homeschool materials at home, can be a huge challenge. We have limited space, so had to be very resourceful in finding the space we needed to accommodate materials in our home.

Storage Solutions for Materials

There are lots of little tricks for storing things like nomenclature and print materials, available online. Some solutions are very elaborate, and others so simple. I have tried many different solutions, and have returned to simple DIY methods. There are many beautiful cabinets and methods that you will see online, but again keep in mind that some of these solutions are for class size use, and must be inherently durable to withstand this kind of use. You will find popular images online of cabinets and drawers for reading series work, grammar, and math, and I fell in love with the images of this amazing storage and tried some in our home. The most important thing to keep in mind; is that keeping things organized in a way that makes sense to you is key. I also found that money could easily be spent in access; for short term storage solutions. In a classroom this organization is crucial to long term survival of materials through years of class interaction, but not so much for home use. The materials turn over fairly quickly at home, so for us in the end simple was far better.

Where can I buy Montessori Materials?

Purchasing Montessori materials can be confusing, and the best options are usually found online. There is great debate in terms of material quality, from those who claim some retailers offer higher quality premium materials, while others sell two lines of quality; an economy line, and a premium line. Generally the difference may be found in the type of wood, or types of beads that are used during manufacturing. Some manufacturers use glass or wooden beads, but the majority use plastic beads. You will find that price can hugely vary depending on the retailer, and the quality they claim to offer. I kept a spread sheet of the materials I was looking for, and a list of who offered them at what price; I also noted shipping costs.

The products that are available from different retailers, can vary quite a bit as well. For instance bead bar colours can slightly, or greatly differ between retailers. We purchased part of our bead cabinet materials from one retailer, but needed to confirm when purchasing the rest at a less expensive retailer, to try and ensure that the colours would match. This is important when you are mixing materials from one retailer to the next for certain materials, but not for the majority.

We did not purchase premium materials, for our use at home. I can tell you that the materials we did purchase were all amazing quality, and we have loved using them; that being said, if you wish to spend the extra dollars on premium materials that is your choice. I can completely understand the expenditure for class use, given the numbers of children and years of use that they will get. Some retailers offer resin versions of some bead materials i.e., the introduction to the decimal system, in golden beads. Resin bead bars, squares, and cubes that are poured into a form, and the beads look like they are connected with plastic; they are also a great less expensive option. Below you can see some of our elementary math materials that are all economy grade.

BUYING MONTESSORI MATERIALS

The question of shipping materials?

We have received tons of questions about shipping options, and really the answer depends greatly upon where you live. We are a Canadian family living close to a border crossing, so we can order our materials online, and have them shipped to a receiver cross border, to save money.

The shipping costs for the materials can be absolutely astounding, and are a huge barrier for some individuals to acquire the materials. It's hard to justify shipping charges that become more than the materials you are hoping to purchase sadly.
The materials are large and heavy, so it is slightly understandable why there can be greater cost. However sometimes the cost is still very large for smaller items.

We have purchased Montessori Materials from many notable companies online including: Kid Advance (the majority of our purchases), IFit, The Montessori Outlet, Adena, Alison's and a few others. I have not made purchases from the other extremely expensive retailers. I cannot tell you where to purchase your materials, but I can tell you I have had very good luck with quality goods, at a greater savings from all of the above. Everything we purchased was wonderful quality; though I have read varying opinions also on all of the above, I think you need to price out and compare. Bulk purchasing your materials where you can, will help you save money. Some retailers offer free shipping after a certain amount has been spent, which can really help.

When I could, I took advantage of bulk ordering to save on shipping. Montessori materials make great Birthday and Christmas gifts, to help you afford this journey.

The other thing to think about, is to consider what you really need and wish to have very carefully before you make the purchase. Once you have read through this entire book and take some time to digest it, you will have a far greater understanding of the sequence and use of the materials, to help you make these decisions.

My advice is to shop around! Most materials are purchased online from various retailers, and are available now on amazon.

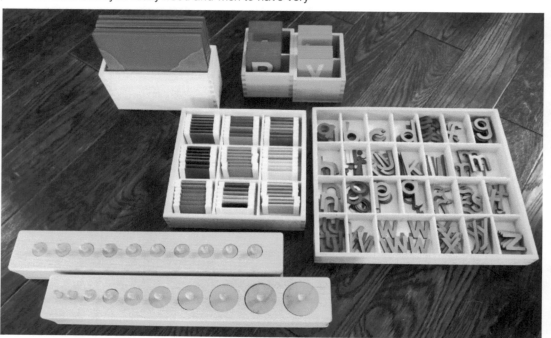

BUYING MONTESSORI MANUALS/ALBUMS

A Practical Guide to Montessori & Homeschooling

Where can I buy Montessori Manuals?

This is also a question that we are often asked. Quite honestly purchasing manuals is not an easy task, for most of us who are homeschooling. Manuals can greatly differ depending on who is offering them. The most prohibitive factor is cost, and shipping. Physical manuals or albums (as you often will hear them called) are large, heavy and numerous, making them extremely expensive to ship; especially for those who do not live in the US. Digital manuals are going to be more economical. The manuals that we use can be found on online, and are now available as a digital option. We have included lots of links on our website, along with other links that we found useful when starting out. Our manuals are amazing, but were one of the sets that lacked visuals, or a great deal of practical information about the materials; they did have amazing detailed lessons, and we needed to make this decision based on cost.

Manuals differ greatly in terms of who is producing them, believe it or not. Teachers and institutes all feel strongly about the content they are producing, and feel that their albums and training are the most serviceable. Some manuals share only lessons with little philosophy and insight; while others are a little better in this regard, but are beyond reach in terms of expense. Some offer detailed lessons, but with very little in terms of photographs for you to easily see how the materials are used.

Manuals are generally divided by Infant and Toddler, Early 3-6, Elementary one 6-9, and Elementary two 9-12. Many subjects are taught concurrently; math and language are sequentially followed in order, but some subjects intermingle in terms of timeline of introduction.

The main thing is that no matter what manuals you are able to acquire, it's important to research and read as much as you can about the materials and method. I have spent years reading and researching, and observing the Montessori community as a whole trying to decipher all that I had questions for. The community online is a very mixed, and sometimes a very divided community. Some are very hard lined purists who believe they have the best training, and that no one should use the method who does not have their training. Please don't let this deter or discourage you! Look at these people for who they are, and give them the benefit in that they are obviously deeply passionate about the method; no matter how un-Montessori like their behavior may be. You will find many who will be helpful, and encouraging.

My hope is that after reading this book you will be far better equipped to find solutions that work for you, and your family. While this book is not a manual, it will help you understand the philosophy, and the entire materials scope and sequence. My hope is that this book will answer the vast majority of questions that you may have had, *AND* offer a great deal of information regarding a huge range of questions that you never knew you had.

Finding lesson information is believe it or not, one of the easier things to find. Thankfully a vast number of individuals have created amazing online video instruction, to help you see exactly how materials are used. Take a good look at the manuals that are offered online, and after reading through you will be able to recognize the materials, and how they are used in practical terms.

The manuals you choose (if any) will depend on what you are able to spend, or if in the end you deem it worth the money given the amount of available information online.

Why are material presentations so methodical?

There are a few components in terms presenting lessons or materials to your child. Depending on what it is you are introducing, and at what stage in the curriculum you are at. There is an initial introduction for a physical material like the Pink Tower, including a demonstration as to how to transport the material to and from the work area. Early traditional material presentations can look quite lengthy, and very dry. In a class environment this methodical repetition is part of the exercise of developing patience, organization, and care for the environment; this is all a fundamental part of the lesson. If your child is working with a material it's important to let them make mistakes and discoveries, we need not point out their mistakes; making mistakes is part of the natural learning process.

You can decide at home what part of initial presentations will work well for your child, without limiting them or their excitement for the material. Generally I introduced our children to new materials and modeled work/play with the material. Our children generally jumped in to explore, and I was so happy to see this. In our self directed home environment we encouraged our children to use the materials, and see where their exploration took them. I did not need to build and take down all materials in order for them to reach the conclusion that a tower could be built with the pink blocks, as this was an amazing discovery that they made on their own. One of the most important things to understand is that exploration and discovery, are the keys to learning.

I did feel it important (as with all things that we live with in our home environment) that I modeled care and respect for the materials, as with all of our belongings.

THREE PERIOD LESSON

A Practical Guide to Montessori & Homeschooling

What is a 3 Period Lesson?

The Montessori 3 Period Lesson is quite simple, and one of the corner stones to presenting early activities to children.

The three components:

Period 1 Naming "*This is an apple*", showing the child

Period 2 Recognition "*Give/show me the apple*", question for the child

Period 3 Pronunciation and recall of the word "*What is this*?, pointing to the apple

There are amazing explanations, lessons and videos online to help you see the Three Period Lesson in action.

What is the purpose?

The 3 period lesson is used when introducing new concepts and ideas to children. Most often used in the 3-6 age range; it helps to introduce new vocabulary in a fun engaging way. It is amazing how much it helps to aide language retention, and recognition of objects. While working with sensorial materials it is used to help your child evaluate differences in materials physically like, thin, thinner, thinnest block etc.

An example of the three period lesson using either images, or real vegetables.

"This is" - "This is broccoli", "This is a green pepper", "This is a tomato"

"Show me/point to" - "Can you show me broccoli?", "Can you point to the green pepper?", " Can you show me the tomato?"

"Ask - What is this?" - Point (or pick up) to the broccoli, Point to the green pepper, Point to the tomato

Why are trays used for Montessori work?

Montessori work trays are often seen in blog posts, school images, manuals, and on retailer sites. The trays are used to house individual activities/work, on one tray. This helps to contain and organize the work for the child. The contents of the tray can easily be carried to the work surface, and in turn replaced. You can use whatever you like; keeping in mind that it needs to be of a size easily carried by a child, and not too heavy. Dollar stores often have great inexpensive trays, and baskets are also often used.

Small baskets and containers are used and reused, for so many activities. It's nice to have several sets that are easily available to present activities.

What are 3 Part Card Trays?

3 Part card trays are small trays with three compartments, to hold a set of 3 Part Cards. These simply keep the images and labels nicely contained, so that they can be neatly presented on the shelf for use. They promote organization, and concentration as your child will separate and return the cards to their home on the tray and shelf.

RUGS FOR WORK

Why are rugs used for Montessori work?

Montessori rugs are often small standard 24" x 36" rugs used for floor work, but also can be used on tables. Maria Montessori (in her handbook) described that the rugs to be used, may be in various colours: red, blue, pink, green or brown. The rugs provide a defined work area that is soft for the materials to be placed on. The rug helps the child to keep their work organized, and to help others know that this is their work space. Rugs for home use make sense also because they help to protect your tables and floor from damage; especially when using things like the Pink Tower that are larger and weigh a fair amount when toppling over.

Rugs of this size can be purchased in many places, and they can usually be found for under $5. Some will say that you must use solid coloured rugs without pattern to avoid distraction, and others feel the "style" of the rug to be less important.

I will tell you my criteria for the rugs we use. I did opt for a little less pattern, because I wanted the activities easily visible on the background. A really busy pattern or super dark color, can make it harder to see the cards or objects etc. I love the little cream background rag rugs (flat woven), with simple stripes. Our children used the stripes to line up work, and these rugs were very inexpensive and easy to find locally. We also used yoga mats, because they are so amazing and soft to use. The choice is yours!

We store our rugs in a large tall container close to areas where they like to work. Children are given lessons early on to practice rolling and unrolling their own rugs, to give them care and control of their work environment. The knobbed Cylinders (to the left) are perfect floor work due to their weight and size.

Why do children work on the floor?

Often you will see children in pictures working on the floor; when you are at home this is entirely up to you, and your child. Working on the floor seems like a natural thing to do for children. Often the early work materials can be large and heavy, so it can be easier and more practical to work on the floor. Some work is very spread out, and requires many components that may easily fall to the floor. Our children love to work at the table, and sometimes even sitting on the table! I was less concerned with where, as opposed to happy productive time with activities. Very often though they do prefer to work on the floor, however in our house we do both.

THREE PART CARDS

A Practical Guide to Montessori & Homeschooling

What are 3 Part Cards?

Three part cards are a set of two identical cards that are cut into three parts. One card contains an image and label, and the second a duplicate image which has the label portion cut from the bottom. Elementary versions sometimes have a definition printed on the label, or on an additional label.

What is the purpose?

The cards are used in 3-6; straight through elementary. Early lessons with the cards start with image to image matching (for children who are not reading), image and label matching (readers or non), label to image matching (readers), and later definition to image matching for elementary, or kids who are able to read the information on the definition cards.

Often three part cards are created in blackline or black and white images. Parts of the image are highlighted or contrasted in colour. Some as you see below, have parts that are denoted with arrows.

The curriculum is very unique in that all facts, information, and concepts are isolated and explained in proper terminology to children. The materials build upon themselves and additional information is revealed through time. Your child's first experience with the cards will be a visual one, and information will follow in stages.

Can I make these?

You can make these cards yourself in a variety of ways. If you are handy on the computer you can make them in Microsoft Word, and this is the easiest as most people have Word on their computer. I create all of our cards in Microsoft Publisher. You can also cut out your cards, hand write the labels, and add images that you either print or cut out from old magazines, flyers, old books, or your own photos. You can laminate them if you wish; it's entirely up to you. If you are short on time or do not wish to make them, do a quick search online for the cards you are looking for. There is a vast assortment of cards available for free, or very inexpensively.

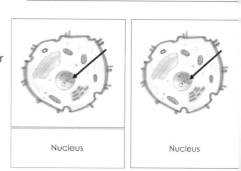

Nucleus   Nucleus

We made our 3 Part Card pouches/ folders very simply; with cardstock folded and stapled to make the pockets that separated and held the cards.

What are Nomenclature Booklets?

Nomenclature booklets usually accompany a set of nomenclature 3 part cards. Nomenclature means, a series of objects or things pertaining to a topic. For example: instrument nomenclature, features a different instrument on each set of three part cards.

What is the purpose?

The books are similar to your definition cards (that are sometimes included with three part cards), but in booklet form and may contain more detailed information. You will typically not find any vocabulary or concepts that are not completely explained, for example: the words "Solar System", would never be used without explaining what that is.

Can I make these?

You can make the booklets on your computer with a bit of research, and using Microsoft Word or the program of your choice. You can also hand write your booklets. It is most popular and easy to purchase them from Montessori printable makers, or to find books that relate to the subjects your child is interested in. Many homeschoolers are offering free booklets that you can print online. I have made printed booklets in three different ways. One is to cut the pages, and staple them together. Another is to cut the pages and place them into a duo tang style folder that you cut down into a smaller size. Finally, I have really liked laminating the pages and hole punching the upper left corner, to place a key or shower curtain ring for more of a flip style book.

If you have more than one child in different age ranges, one child can use the 3 Part Cards while the older child reads the booklet to them.

Fungus

Stapled

Ring

Duo Tang or Project Folder Method

PRINT MATERIAL MAKING

Tips for making print materials?

If you are going to be printing and making your own print materials, here is a list of tools I have found incredibly handy to have.

Laminator: I bought an inexpensive laminator for $29, and lamination pockets on amazon. They were by far the most economical option that I found. I would highly recommend this investment at some point, if you are going to produce any amount of print materials on your own.

Paper Cutter: I began with a really cheap paper cutter that I purchased for around $11, and I do have to invest in replacement blades from time to time. I initially thought this was a waste of money, until I spent a massive amount of time trying to cut out everything by hand.

Printer: A printer of course; I use a cheap printers because I have purchased many printers that were expensive, middle of the road, or cheap, and experienced very little difference in the longevity and quality for what I was looking to create. I have also had many things printed from a local office supply store.

Short & Long arm Stapler: Staplers are really indispensable for material making. The long arm stapler, allows you the extra length needed to create simple books & booklets. We often made small plain paper booklets for so many activities.

I think the most important thing that learned was that I didn't need all of the materials at once; nor did I need everything that I found, or watched others use online. I found it extremely easy to get carried away, by all of the incredible materials that I was finding. The most valuable print materials that I made and used often, were materials that I needed to work directly with the Montessori materials we were using. At home my children used geography, language and math printables very regularly, but many others were rarely used. This will depend on your children and what they are interested in, and also the amount of time you wish to expend.

I laminated most of our early print materials for durability. I liked the way it made them look, and how easy they were to manipulate. I selectively laminated many later materials, because they were not used so repetitively.

MONTESSORI HOME CLASSROOM

A Practical Guide to Montessori & Homeschooling

What does a Montessori homeschool space look like?

This depends on the family. Some Montessori homeschool rooms look much like a classroom, while others contain only some elements of a classroom. The common characteristics of a Montessori space include low completely accessible shelving, baskets, a selection of materials, and great organization. Some use many traditional materials, and others use the philosophy to create Montessori inspired work; meaning work that is specifically targeted at certain skills, and with an element of self- correction.

Do I need a Montessori Classroom setup at home to be successful?

I think not, however some feel that you do and others do not. When we were starting I did my very best to stay away from any information that tried to define this experience for me, and tell me what my experience "should" look like. If you have the space and want a classroom in your home, then you should try it. I do feel though that you should make these decisions based on your family, your space, and your needs. I know it can be hard when you visit all of these beautiful spaces online, and feel like you "should" recreate this literal translation of a Montessori Classroom at home. For some this works well, and for others not at all.

There is a great deal on the internet about creating a Montessori space at home, and I would encourage you to think about the following:

This is Maria Montessori's description of the children's house, and I would keep this in your mind, when you think about your home and your children.
This is synapsis of Maria Montessori's Description of a "Children's House (early school or classroom)" as written in her book "*Maria Montessori's Own Hand Book*"

"*The "Children's House" is the environment which is offered to the child that he may be given the opportunity to develop his activities.*"

"*It ought to be a **real house**; a set of rooms with a garden. A garden with shelters because children can play or sleep under them, also bring their tables out to work under them. In this they may live almost entirely in the open air.*"

"*In the principle room (working room), a very long cupboard with large doors, it is very low. Inside the cupboard is kept the didactic materials (Montessori materials as we know them today).*"

"*The special characteristic of the equipment of these houses is that it is adapted for children, <u>not adults</u>.*"

"*The furniture is light so that the children can move it, there are low tables, small chairs, small wicker armchairs and sofas.*"

There is so much more to read in her description, and I would encourage you to read it for yourself. This is the environment she described, and she also describes it as a miniature family. This truly is all you need, in an effort to organize a beautiful space for your children. We did create a Montessori inspired classroom in our home, and I discuss this in the book and why we changed it. However because there is great interest about this space and so many questions, I will show you a few images in the coming pages.

MONTESSORI HOME CLASSROOM

Our Former Montessori Inspired Homeschool Space

Foldable Table & Chairs, small stools, all tall bookcases are from Ikea

All low shelves are stacking shoe shelves, from a discount retailer

MONTESSORI CURRICULUM

Does Montessori go by grade?

Montessori is not grade based, but rather based on child development. There are three planes of development that you can equate to a mainstream grade school curriculum, by the age of the child. Early Childhood 3-6 years of age, Elementary 1 (6-9) years of age, and Elementary 2 (9-12) years of age.

Does Montessori use testing?

Montessori is not a curriculum that uses tests to grade children. You may find some schools that are in need to *comply* with standardized testing, and this is dependent on where they are located.

Early Childhood Montessori materials have a build in element of self-correction, that helps your child to maintain confidence, and self-reliance. There is nothing more powerful than having the ability to identify your own errors, and to correct them. For example: most materials have some form of marking system (stickers or colored dots) on the bottom or back of materials. If the object/card/material has been correctly matched, then the sticker/dot/letter/number will match; thus providing a very effective method for the child to track their own progress.

Montessori work is targeted to individual children and their needs, and their progress is documented on an entirely different level than in mainstream education. In schools or at home progress tracking may look like this for example: you will know every letter and sound that your child knows, every materials they have worked with, and children progress at their own pace when they are ready. The method makes testing insignificant, because children know the material so well before they progress; and after all isn't this really about the child? Testing in mainstream really has little to do with the actual wellbeing of a child, and more to do with providing a measure to ensure teachers are doing their job. In Early and Upper Elementary, some form of quizzing for various materials or concepts that the child has worked with may be involved. Should your child choose higher education or training, there are many classes online or otherwise that can help your child with the process of testing.

Exploring constellations, Age 3 & 6

How can I create a feeling of community that is found in a Montessori class, at home?

There are many things to keep in mind when you are thinking about Montessori homeschooling, or any style of homeschooling/unschooling. Classrooms are multi age, and often the children work in groups. This can happen at home, but the reality is often your child will be working on their own at home, or with you. This is not a bad thing, it's just different. In a classroom the director/directress/teacher/guide presents activities and guidance as needed, and at home our experience was much different. While we follow our children in their interests, we are also extremely involved. We are down on the floor playing games (not just Montessori), and working through activities as interest should arise *with* our children. It is more often than not that our children want to be/play with us, and it was extremely important to us to make this happen, as you are your child's community at home. Home learners also have great relationships and ties within their greater community. There is opportunity in most areas, for your child to be involved in activities/classes with large numbers of children every day of the week, should they so desire. Home learning communities are growing daily, and really the opportunities are endless.

How much should I put on my shelves? What do I do if my child doesn't want to do the activities?

I wish I could answer this question in a simple straight forward way, however so much depends on what you are trying to accomplish at home. It's helpful to know how a class environment works, and how your home is so much more than this type of environment.

We managed our expectations a little differently at home, in that we presented many materials as games during periods of interest. We played the games and worked on activities around things that our children loved, and were interested in. If they did not wish to do an activity it was often that the work was presented too early, or not during a period of interest. Remember that you are not limited in any form to what you have prepared in your home. As a home learner you can get up and go; go to a museum, go to a library, organize a class with other like-minded children, or take a road trip to explore.

A Montessori classroom may start the year with little on their shelves, and there are a few things to keep in mind as to how this translates to a home environment. Montessori classrooms are like mainstream schools, in that a child is required to spend a set number of hours (in most cases) in the classroom. The activities/materials are the main focus because this is the purpose of the class; in contrast to a home environment. The children will most likely gravitate to certain activities over others. As the year progresses new materials are added to the shelves, and the class works through them. Interest will be peaked as new materials are added, taking brilliant advantage of curiosity. Classrooms are carefully crafted and prepared, to provide the children with the feeling of choice, and self direction. In reality the choice still lies in what is available to the child within that room/building/shelf.

At home we have found that it took little time for our children to acquire new skills and concepts, if they were ready and interested. In our real life environment we did not need to structure time limits, or periods to work. We were not in a scheduled school environment, where such measures must be in place to manage large groups of children. We do not interrupt their work/play unless we have a scheduled appointment, and this too is part of the learning. There will be great opportunity to help your children understand scheduled time through appointments, sports, classes, music lessons, TV shows, and even simple activities like getting to the movie theater on time.

MONTESSORI HOMESCHOOLING

Do I have to be a teacher to use the Montessori curriculum?

In my opinion obviously, I would say no. At the end of the day (for me) I would say that the basic content of any curriculum is just curriculum. The difference is that the Montessori curriculum is chronological in all aspects, and very in-depth. It is presented to a child in a unique way, and it helps to have a holistic understanding of the approach. The philosophy meant so much more to me, than my children learning or mastering facts. I was most concerned with seeing my children for who they were as individuals, and meeting their needs. I think that understanding the principles of positive parenting and creating a harmonious home environment; rich with hands on learning, interaction, love and respect, were our guiding principles. The Montessori philosophy of complete equality for children, creating an environment to facilitate self-reliance, to celebrate a child's individual pursuits and passion for learning, was/is and always will be our goal. I think that if you understand this part, you will be very successful whether you use Montessori materials and lessons, or not. This curriculum and philosophy was so carefully crafted in meeting the developmental needs of children, that if you really understand the philosophy (in my opinion) you will be sitting at the beginning of a beautiful journey with your family. That being said using the materials and understanding how they work together, does require research and practice. You can do this in smaller bites though, as it can be so overwhelming. Montessori teachers have had the benefit of countless hours working with, and understanding the materials and that is an incredible advantage; but you can do this - just go slowly and truly observe your child, in an effort to see and understand how they interact with their environment. Make this experience yours!

So there is a flip side to this; can you use the materials without the philosophy? Yes I think you can, and many people do. The materials are amazing in and of themselves as manipulatives and aids for other curricula, and I talk more about my thoughts on this in the tutoring section.

Is Montessori for gifted children?

Montessori was not created for gifted children, though Montessori meets the needs of all children given the guiding principles of following the child, and understanding their needs and development. If your child requires a greater length of time to understand a concept you simply work at their pace. If they are loving their work and are passionate about it, then continue to explore!

Early Fractions Introduction, Age 5

MONTESSORI RECORD KEEPING

How does Montessori track my child's progress?

There is an extensive amount of recording through observation of your child that happens in a Montessori school environment. The types of records kept will depend on where the school is located, and whether they are a private school or public. None the less, the development and learning for every child is tracked extensively, and individually. Tracking is done either traditionally handwritten, or with programs designed for this purpose; remember, a school is answering to paying parents and officials for potentially large groups of children. The amount of tracking and recording that you do at home will depend on where you live, and what may be required of you by the school authorities where you reside.

The vast majority of families who have embarked on the homeschooling journey have a very deep connection to their child and their daily development, and acquisition of developmental and intellectual skills. Should documentation be required, it is usually fairly easy to prepare any required documentation in great detail given the amount of time you spend with your child on an individual basis.

Each plane of development has a detailed list of skills and materials that the child has explored, and such records are available online to be printed if you wish to track your children in this way. A Montessori teacher/guide is fully aware of what the child has experienced and worked with, and to the degree they understand the material - as you will at home. The most important thing in a child's work with a material, is that they develop an understanding of the process and operation, as opposed to mere memorization of facts.

For example in Early Education recording at home could look like the following:

Language 3-6

Has worked with Sandpaper Letters a,b,c,d,e,f,g,h,I,j,k,l, and so on.

Has grasped the sound for Letters a,b,c,d,e,f,g,h,I,j,k,l, and so on. Each letter being recorded as the child has worked with or developed the skill.

In Early and Upper Elementary though while recording through observation and through interaction with your child, the directress/director will work with your child to understand their level of retention. Often the student will teach other students, and demonstrate lessons back to their teacher/guide. This may look like a quiz, but to the student it is just part of the wonder and excitement of the material they are learning. Students may also create a portfolio of their work, and you can do this at home as well if you like.

At home my son was so very excited to "teach" us a lesson or concept he had worked with, and in turn his younger sister. It takes little else to observe what the child is absorbing and learning. We've chosen to keep a detailed photographic record of our home learning journey, and of course I write about it as you know. This was more than sufficient for the area in which we live. You may be required to submit a more formal layout to your school board/authority. There are many websites available now to help you understand and formulate the paperwork, in a format that a school board needs to see (if applicable). Often you will be provided paperwork to complete depending on your location.

The self-directed home environment is so unique and specific to your child. I found it easy to recant our children's skills, and worked to never let the process of documentation and over planning get in the way of our children's self-directed natural learning; at home you have this advantage.

MONTESSORI VS. MAINSTREAM ED

What is the difference between Montessori and mainstream curricula?

This will depend greatly upon where you are from. There is a vast difference between a Montessori school environment, and a mainstream environment. Mainstream classes are teacher directed, driven, and focused. Children are measured by grade; with great comparison to their peers. Most are classified by grades, with corresponding ages. Most classes are comprised of one or sometimes two grades per class, while maintaining separation. The mainstream curriculum itself, is an overview of skills and tasks to be attained, and measured by age. The curriculum is created in each class by a teacher who is following a standard formula for education. The teacher decides what materials and topics will be taught, and to their degree of satisfaction and ability. The materials and degree of coverage, can change from teacher to teacher, from year to year. A teacher can be placed in a classroom to teach material they have never taught, thus needing to create materials and resources for their new class. Mainstream depends upon who is teaching where and when. You could have a completely progressive teacher filled with energy and passion, but if they do not arrive to an environment supportive of this; then the environment and students suffer. Progressive education and alternatives can be hindered by individuals, and schoolboards.

Montessori class rooms are multi aged communities of children, who work together. The Montessori curriculum is very broad and begins with Early Education 3-6 years of age, the next being 6-9, followed by Elementary 9-12 years. Many Montessori environments also include infant and toddler programs, and the information available to read about these young environments, are so valuable for new/all parents. Each class is equipped with materials, and referred to as the *prepared environment*. The materials all have a place and purpose, in an overall holistic approach to learning. Meaning that the materials have commonalities, in that they are worked in unison with a child's needs and natural development.

All areas of the classroom are taught with a scientific principle, or method of exploration and evaluation, to be carried out by your child. The teacher/Directress/guide tends to the prepared environment, imparts initial lessons, and observes a child carrying out their work. The teacher will provide guidance where needed.

The classrooms have a set curriculum of subjects Early Education 3-6 age range is divided into the following, Practical Life, Sensorial, Language, Mathematics, Geography, Fractions, Geometry, Zoology, Botany 6-9 years, and 9-12 years cover materials for Language, Mathematics, Geography, History, Fractions, Geometry, Zoology, Botany , Biology, Geology, Physics and Chemistry.

Each subject has a complete curriculum based on the complete history and science of the subject with prepared materials, manipulatives and experiments, literature, and resources etc.

Every school and teacher has a set of manuals, or manuals they have created for teaching. All subjects that are historically, and scientifically accurate and complete. Most importantly every teacher has vast understanding of child development, as the curriculum is completely founded upon it. Children progress through the prepared environment at their own pace, and move further as their development dictates. The success of the child is not measured nor dictated by that of their peers, though given the nature of the materials and sensitivity of the environment, it would be evident if a child were struggling.

WORK BOOKS & PRINTABLES

Are work books used in Montessori?

The traditional Montessori Curriculum does not use work books or worksheets that you often see in mainstream curriculums; though they do work with a vast number of printed materials. In Early Education the Montessori Method is a hands on concrete experience. Your child works with, evaluates, and experiments with a range of materials and manipulatives in Language, Sensorial, Mathematics, Botany, Zoology, Practical Life and Cultural/Geography subjects.

As your child develops the curriculum develops alongside them to meet their developmental and intellectual needs. The curriculum progresses from concrete materials, to more abstract learning and printed materials. Printed materials differ in that they are created to isolate concepts, and specific topics for learning; in contrast workbooks often have many things printed on one page. The child completes a small section or so on, "Nouns" for example, and quickly moves to another topic usually with very little exploration and actual insight to what they have really learned, or how it applies in their everyday environment. Some workbook publishers are producing better quality content, which in some instances may complement your materials. Materials like this are often used in mainstream classes, because they are easily tracked for proof (or disprove) that your child is working in class. Montessori materials are designed *for* a child, to completely have freedom to explore a topic without distraction or pressure to move on to another "page", or to be graded.

What are printables, and how are they used in Montessori?

There are a large range of printables to accompany Montessori Materials. Montessori printables are very different from many mainstream curriculum printables, and are used to solidify or aid a topic in a visually interesting way. They are specifically formatted to isolate topics, and deliver information in a sequence. Most Montessori printables are laminated, cut apart, and used as a manipulative in a number of ways. The other form of printables often seen in homes, are those that can be used in place of the traditional manipulatives. There are many areas of the curriculum where printed versions of the actual traditional materials can be more economical, and make very good sense for many at home. This is especially true of elementary materials. Early on a hands on sensorial experience with the materials is so very important, however at home you can use a combination of Montessori materials and other products. Later for lower and upper elementary, there are some fantastic options for printed materials. We have created many that are available on our printables site. For many at home, a good mix of print and traditional materials can help make Montessori far more affordable.

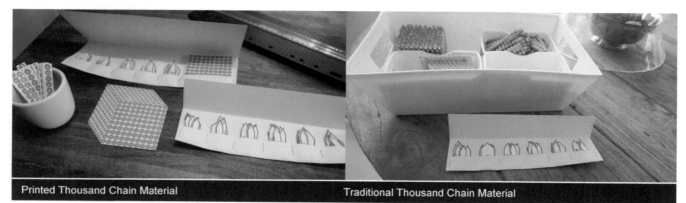

Printed Thousand Chain Material | Traditional Thousand Chain Material

Printables vs. Traditional Material

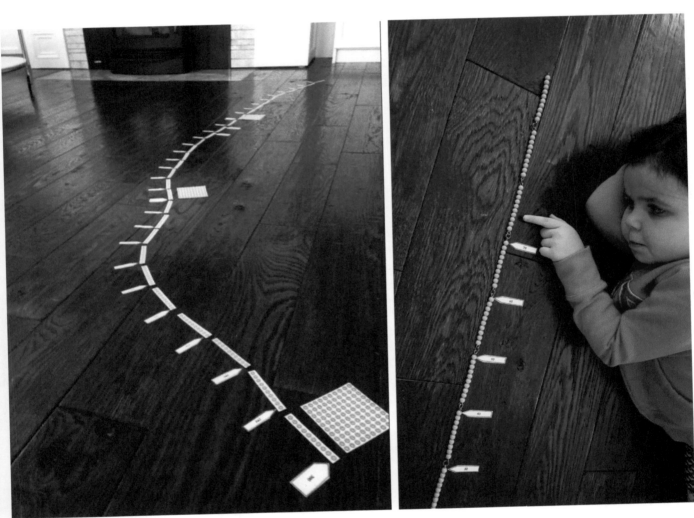

I am asked all the time about my top bead choices and picks. I talk about my choices and what I would have done differently in hindsight throughout the book, while talking about each material. I strongly believe in a mix of materials; especially DIY solutions for ease of storage, affordability, and practicality at home.

MONTESSORI TUTORING

Can Montessori be used for after school tutoring?

Given the hands on nature of Montessori Materials, I have always felt that they are a wonderful option to demonstrate concepts along with your mainstream curriculum. Many curricula have adopted Montessori principles and manipulatives, to accompany lessons and activities. You will find many video tutorials online, to help you present concepts with the materials to your child. The materials are expensive so often using just a few materials, and perhaps some of the printable and DIY versions may be a good option for you. Most early materials are wonderful to incorporate.

Can I start with Montessori and then move to another curriculum?

This happens often in mainstream education. In many areas there appear to be far more Early Education Montessori schools then elementary. Very often children start in Casa De Bambini "Children's House" 0-6, and then enter a mainstream school. It is always interesting to me to hear the number of people who think that Montessori is a preschool education only, not even knowing there *is* Montessori Elementary. Many report that there is a transition period of adjustment for a child who moves from Montessori to main stream & vice versa; due to the move from the materials, and multi age open atmosphere that they had experienced in a Montessori Classroom. I feel that change can be difficult no matter the circumstances. Many who change from one to the other, work closely with their schools and teachers to create as smooth of a transition as possible. So yes it is done often, and hopefully with care and consideration.

Can I combine Montessori with other curricula at home?

Yes as mentioned above in tutoring you can. As a homeschooler do what is best for your child, and use the materials to your child's advantage or to enhance what you are already doing in your home.

Can I begin Montessori with an older child?

Fraction Materials are a great add in for tutoring work

You can certainly begin the Montessori Method with an older child. There are certain areas of the curriculum that are best to work with, in sequence. Take a good look at each section, and see where your child fits in terms of their academic knowledge. If I were to jump in with my older child I would begin language and math (no matter the age) at Elementary 1, as well as all other subjects. The curriculum is interesting and fun, and completely scale-able to adjust where you need it to. You can move really quickly if you need to, in an effort to follow your child, or slow things down accordingly. Never be afraid to start anything based on age. Also take advantage of as many DIY materials as you can, and adjust materials to the interests of your child.

MONTESSORI HOME ORGANIZATION

How do I organize my home to be Montessori friendly, and what does that mean?

Montessori is not just about a curriculum, and a set of materials. Montessori is about loving and nurturing your children on their journey to becoming independent, self-reliant, knowledge seeking, productive, and happy individuals.

No one person can tell you how to organize your home, because your home and needs will be unique to your family.

I will tell you what we kept in mind and heart, as our children grew. We were constantly re-evaluating our living areas to meet the needs of our children, and family.

We do our very best to provide an environment that meets their interests, and is accessible to our children. Think of the needs of any person who may have certain accessibility requirements, and apply that same love and forethought to your child's environment.

We provided small tables and chairs, for crafting and creating. We organized games and puzzles on low shelves, for our children to retrieve and easily return them.

We placed snacks and dishes, in places that they could easily reach. Their books were on low shelves. Clothing was easily accessible in their lowest drawers. Outer wear is kept on low hooks at the door etc.

The principles of accessibility, also apply to our outdoor environment. We have child sized gardening tools, and basic (child size) tools are available, when they work on building projects with us. We have smaller outdoor chairs and tables etc.

Everything that our children need to meet their basic needs, is available to help foster independence and freedom. Our spaces are constantly evolving and in a state of change, as is our lives.

An environment that is not accessible to your child becomes frustrating, and hinders their freedom and independence.

An environment without accessibility creates dependence.
How frustrating would this be for you?

Are Montessori Materials toys?

Montessori Materials were designed with specific careful purpose to work with the Montessori curriculum that is based on natural child development. Maria Montessori was not a toy maker, and referred to play as a child's work. Maria Montessori spoke about toys quite frankly and my interpretation of her words is this; a toy can never take the place of real world experience for a child. In other words giving a child a play kitchen, can never replace the benefit of a child who is provided the opportunity to work with their own tools in a real kitchen etc., and I wholeheartedly believe this to be true. However I feel that a child can have both real world, and creative expression through play with toys. The child will always seek out real experiences, and we need to recognize, respect, and help to fill this need. We can help to accomplish this through an accessible environment

It is easy to see why many refer to Montessori materials as toys. There are so many wooden toys and puzzles on the market today that have similar characteristics of Montessori materials. In our home our children view Montessori materials as tools of exploration, freedom, and learning. We have worked with our children and modeled care and concern for our/their environment, for the things we love to use and play with in our home. *All* of the toys in our home, are treated with equal respect and have thoughtful homes in our environment. This type of care and concern is not limited to Montessori, but for *any toy* that brings interest and excitement to our child.

I would say that our children respect the materials, and interact with them for their intended purpose, but also for the sheer pleasure of their beauty, design and function. Our children do not view them differently from their toys, even if I have an extended knowledge of the materials.

Montessori work in our home *is play*. I believe that this type of exploration and creativity with materials can be explored with any other toy or material you may have in your home, being Montessori or not. The only difference is, its connection to the curriculum as a whole.

Do I need to buy wooden toys only?

My thought has always been to carefully observe my children in effort to meet their needs, development, and interests (see baby toddler section). Many of the toys in our home environment are wooden. We chose them for their beauty, design, and function. We also have large collections of plastic toys. Lego is a fantastic example of an incredible design and construct toy/system.

You need only purchase what you are comfortable purchasing; the choice in yours! **Please consider that children form emotional connections** to their toys and belongings, so while it may feel good to you to purge their toys; it can be so devastating for a child. What if you woke one morning, and all of your most prized belongings were missing? What if your belongings were taken, and given away by someone you *loved and trusted*? Even worse what if they did this right in front of you? I would encourage you to think about your choices in effort to avoid this kind of situation. Our children were always involved with choices in terms of donating, or re-gifting their precious belongings. Consider how it would feel to have your mom pop over and pack up your things, because she felt they were not needed or of value.

Thank you for being here. We will see you in the next book; Homeschooling Basics.

It's a lot to digest, but we will get there together!

~ *Cherine*

A PRACTICAL GUIDE
TO MONTESSORI & HOMESCHOOLING
BOOK COLLECTION

Homeschooling Basics

Homeschooling Basics is an invaluable resource for those who are new to homeschooling, or well rooted. This book covers a broad range of questions about home learning, resources and the logistics of balancing family needs while learning at home. This book supports parents who are looking for solutions to provide a connected and peaceful home learning environment for their children. Homeschooling Basics covers everything from peaceful parenting, home organization solutions, to practical natural learning resources and ideas. We share our home learning story with you, along with many of the challenges and beauty of our home learning experience.

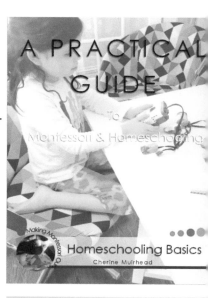

Baby & Toddler

The Baby & Toddler book provides support for parents and caregivers who are beginning their parenting journey or perhaps are looking for a new perspective. This book will help parents and caregivers to create a safe and supportive environment that will work in harmony with the developmental needs of children. This book will offer peaceful non-judgmental parenting strategies, resources and solutions that will support your individual needs and growth as a family. This book provides information on the history and use of Montessori infant toddler mobiles, and extensive DIY tutorials for creating materials and mobiles for your child. Each tutorial is beautifully photographed in full colour providing the steps, templates, and material options for creating your own mobiles inexpensively. This book also covers infant toddler Montessori or inspired materials and toys, and how they support your child's natural development.

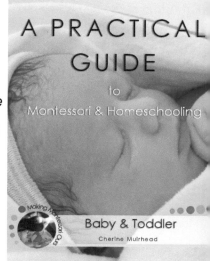

Practical Life

The Montessori Practical Life experience is one of the most beautiful experiences and gifts for any child at home. Children work through this period to build motor skills and knowledge of their environment through investigation and exploration. The activities help to foster natural independence, self-reliance, and self-esteem. The heart of practical life is empowerment through observation, in connecting and fostering the physical and mental developmental needs and well-being of children. It is about creating the space and freedom for a child to interact within their environment. This book will provide ideas and support for those who wish to create a natural and practical environment for children to explore. This book offers a close look at traditional Practical Life materials and trays, and alternatives to support a child's natural curiosity and development through daily living.

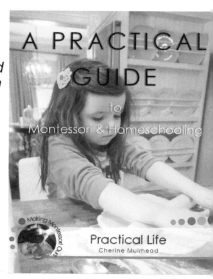

A PRACTICAL GUIDE
TO MONTESSORI & HOMESCHOOLING
BOOK COLLECTION

Sensorial

Early Sensorial is an extraordinary journey that every child will embark on. This book lays out the Montessori Sensorial experience in full colour photography to help you see the materials, function and purpose clearly. The Sensorial basic scope and sequence is explained in a practical and comprehensive way to support parents in understanding how Sensorial materials (in any form) support your child's natural development. Some materials from this collection are used throughout mathematics, and this information is clearly identified in effort to help guide material purchasing choices. This book provides DIY solutions and alternatives to help make the journey into the senses affordable or free. We offer our experience in using the materials at home and how they lived accessibly within our home environment. This book also identifies materials that are carried forth into other areas of the curriculum later on.

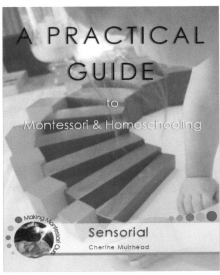

Early Language

The Early Language book is a beautiful full colour exploration of the sequence of early Montessori Language and materials for the three to six age range. Montessori language is a unique hands on exploration of language through the use of physical manipulatives and objects, making it a dynamic interactive experience for children. This book provides extensive information knowledge, tutorials and solutions for affordable language material making. The book supports parents to foster the natural progression of language development through observation in offering materials that meet the needs of their children. The goal of this book is to help parents to identify the components, purpose and use of early Montessori language materials as a guide for those wishing to incorporate these materials as a home learning option.

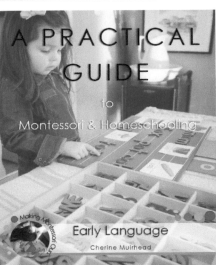

Elementary Language

Elementary Language is a continuation of Early Language. This book covers the sequence of language materials used during the elementary curriculum, six through twelve years of age. All materials are photographed in full colour and provide information as to the components covered, use and purpose of the lessons and materials. This book provides solutions to create inexpensive DIY options for physical and print materials. Grammar materials are covered in great detail.

A PRACTICAL GUIDE
TO MONTESSORI & HOMESCHOOLING
BOOK COLLECTION

Early Math

This is an extensive book that covers the range of three to six years of age. Early Math begins with a concrete, physical exploration of numeracy through beautiful manipulatives and materials. Early Math delivers a fully photographed investigation of these materials, including tutorials for use of all materials and the developmental purpose. This book supports parents in working with the materials in a way in which will enhance their child's natural love and curiosity of the numerical world. This book will identify materials and their supporting components (including print materials) and how they are used together. It also identifies materials that are carried forward into elementary math. This book provides extensive DIY solutions for affordable material making, and alternatives for parents who are looking to support their children with resources who are on a natural learning path. This book benefits parents and caregivers who may be looking to provide additional math resources into their existing environment.

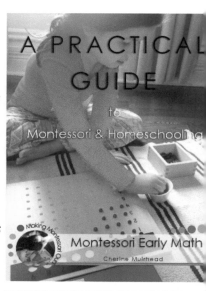

Elementary Math

Elementary Math is a continuation of Early Math. Elementary Math covers the age range of six to twelve years of age. This book covers elementary materials in full colour photography with extensive tutorials for the use and purpose of each material. This book will help parents to support a math journey that is created with a stunning base of manipulative materials and games, to bring more complex math concepts to life in a practical and clear way. Each material section covers DIY solutions and alternatives for parents who may wish to incorporate all or a portion of the materials affordably into their environment.

Early Geography

Early Geography is an incredible world of discovery that supports parents, caregivers and individuals to foster a child's connection to the diversity and beauty of their global community. This book covers the three to six year sequence of early Montessori geography materials through a beautifully photographed full colour experience. In addition this book lays out the elementary sequence, and identifies which materials are carried forward from early to elementary geography. The purpose and use of materials are practically and clearly explained, along with tutorials and alternatives to help create affordable and accessible solutions at home. This book provides support to parents and individuals who may wish to incorporate all or a selection of the materials into their natural learning environment.

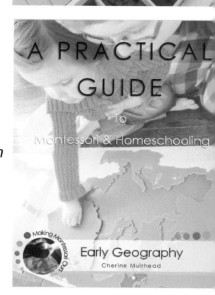

COMING SOON!

A PRACTICAL GUIDE TO MONTESSORI & HOMESCHOOLING
BOOK COLLECTION

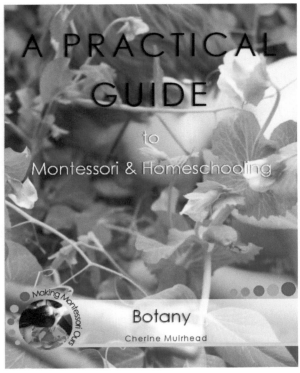

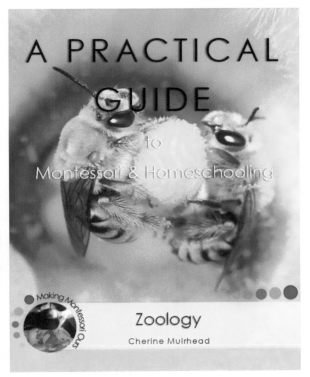

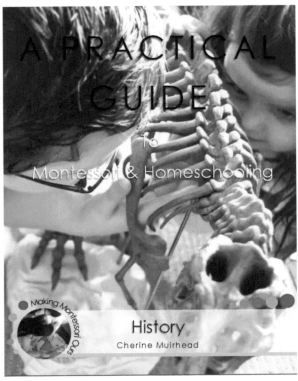

ABOUT THE AUTHOR

Cherine is the mother of two beautiful children, and the author and creator behind Making Montessori Ours. She is a former Director, and Program Coordinator for Children & Families. Cherine has spent the last 12 years at home with her children researching and implementing Montessori Philosophy and Materials, into her full time home learning environment.

She has authored, produced and published a vast collection of Montessori PDF Learning Materials, and with her husband Authored & Illustrated the Ava & Cat Early Reading Series of Children's Books.

A Practical Guide to Montessori & Homeschooling Series, has been born from years of research and practical working knowledge of Montessori Materials, Philosophy and Curriculum in a home learning environment. She has worked to create a complete picture of the practical inner workings of Montessori at home.

Cherine and her husband Gregory are both Artists that produce a collection of artisan jewelry and textiles.

Cherine Muirhead

Connect With Us

You can find us in the following spaces Online:

Site: www.makingmontessoriours.com & www.gcmcraft.com

Shop: www.makingmontessorioursprintables.com

Face Book: https://www.facebook.com/MakingMontessoriOurs/

Pinterest: https://www.pinterest.com/cherinexa/

Instagram: https://www.instagram.com/cherine.muirhead/

Twitter: https://twitter.com/CherineM1

Google +: https://plus.google.com/103279387818959695504